IN OLD PHOTOGRAPHS

BRITAIN

THE CHANGING FACE OF RUNCORN

DAVE THOMPSON

SUTTON PUBLISHING

Sutton Publishing Limited
Phoenix Mill · Thrupp · Stroud
Gloucestershire · GL5 2BU

First published 2004

Title page photograph: These artistic friezes on the waterfront at Mersey Road are a constant reminder that much of Runcorn's 1,000 year history can be traced in the fortunes of its waterways. (*Dave Thompson*)

British Library Cataloguing in Publication Data
A catalogue record for this book is available from the British Library.

ISBN 0-7509-3507-3

Typeset in 10.5/13.5 Photina.
Typesetting and origination by
Sutton Publishing Limited.
Printed and bound in England by
J.H. Haynes & Co. Ltd, Sparkford.

This book is dedicated to the memory of my grandparents, who through their tales of the past unknowingly inspired my love of what went before.

Do you recognise a face from the past? This is party-time at the Cooper Street Mission in 1952. (*Betty Helsby*)

CONTENTS

ACKNOWLEDGEMENTS

The author wishes to acknowledge his appreciation to the many people and organisations who generousl
provided photographs and other factual material for use in this book: Peter Ainsworth, All Saints Schoo
Dave Bettley, Joanne Brown, Terry Burns, June Carrington, Catalyst Museum, John Cook, Ian Douglas, Perc
Dunbavand, John Frodsham, Roy Gough, Denis Hamilton, Halton Borough Council, Highfield Male Voic
Choir – Runcorn, Liz Howard, ICI, Diane Jones, Edna Lea, William Leathwood, Manx National Heritag
Library, Margaret Marsh, the late May Martin, Bob Martindale, Christine McGugan, Paul Meara, Ray Mille
Norton Priory Museum Trust, Omnicolour, Arthur Orchard, Jim Polding, Alan Roberts, Alex Runci
Runcorn Subscription Bowls Club, *Runcorn & Widnes Weekly News*, Mildred Walker, Salt Union, Fre
Terretta, Harry Thompson, *Warrington Guardian*.

Above: Runcorn's civic coat of arms signifies prosperity and commerce and reminds us of many chapters
the town's eventful history. The walled crown represents the ancient stockade built by Princess Ethelfled
The lion is taken from the coat of arms of the Savage family: its crown is a reminder of the local links wi
the monarchy through the Barony of Halton, and the shield with the lion represents the arms of Willia
FitzNigel, the third Baron of Halton. Within the main shield of the arms are shown two flaying knive
reminders of the tanning industry which prospered here for so long. The main emblem of the shield is th
galley ship with the Cheshire sheaf on its sail. This ship and the motto signify a time when Runcorn
prosperity depended heavily upon the local waterways. '*Navem Mercibus Implere*' means to 'fill the ships wi
goods'. (*Halton Borough Council*)

INTRODUCTION

W here once we dwelt our name is heard no more' wrote the poet William Cowper, but within these pages we see the places and scenes around which the names of generations of Runcornians still reverberate. Family albums, newspaper images and professional archives have all merged to provide a portrait of these everyday folk leading their everyday lives – caught for posterity.

We think of Runcorn as an industrial town, with a background rooted in the chemical industry and the waterways, yet for centuries it was nothing more than a pretty, rural hamlet with a scattering of tenements and an ancient parish church. In the early nineteenth century Runcorn's remoteness and idyllic riverfront appearance even gave rise to summer holidaymakers and the establishment of boarding schools. A salt-water bathhouse was built in 1822 and people came from far and wide to enjoy Runcorn waters.

Industrialisation crept slowly at first and was spurred on by the opening of the Bridgewater Canal and the Runcorn to Latchford Canal. Soapworks and sandstone quarries followed and the town's shallow draft port began to blossom, as did fledgling barge and ship-building yards on the Mersey. The Runcorn Hill and Weston quarries fed an almost incessant thirst for stone at Liverpool docks, then emerging as one of the world's great ports. Over time Runcorn also emerged as a prominent place for tanning, and with the opening of the Salt Union and Castner Kellner works the chemical industry established itself as the principal employer for the district throughout the twentieth century.

This book primarily captures the town over the last 150 years and traces the influence and importance of the social and industrial developments that have continuously changed and reshaped the face of Runcorn. The town grew considerably with the opening in 1894 of the Manchester Ship Canal, and the deep draught ports it provided at Runcorn and Weston Point bustled with cargos coming and going from far and wide. New settlers came to the town, particularly swelling the population during the construction of the ship canal, and they brought their own traditions, faiths and entertainment. By 1900 the town had Anglican, Wesleyan and Primitive Methodist, Congregationalist, Roman Catholic and Welsh churches as well as various missions, most of which ran Sunday schools and contributed to the annual Whit walks. Undoubtedly this was Runcorn's most important social occasion, when only the best clothes were worn and where silken banners made a colourful public spectacle. Victorian Runcorn had a close-knit spirit, most evident in its brisk gossipy shops and the plethora of social clubs, entertainment and sporting groups then being established. New communities were formed around hastily built terraced streets; yet the town still retained its quaint corners, like Pool Hollow.

Three great 1,000 ft bridges have crossed the river at Runcorn Gap, each casting an influence on the town's fortunes. The best loved of these is still the old transporter bridge which clattered and banged to and fro across the Mersey for fifty-six years, leaving an indelible mark in the memories of Runcorn's older inhabitants. Life in the town's schools, churches, and work places is also captured in these pages, as are glimpses back at many of the key events and happenings in Runcorn's past. Sporting moments, royal visits, old modes of transport and cherished street scenes have made it into print once more. There is even space to recall the faces of celebrated Runcornians, like Sir Thomas Hall Caine, one of the most distinguished novelists of Victorian times, and Thomas 'Todger' Jones, Runcorn's VC hero. Also captured are scenes from the Second World War when a thankful town escaped relatively unscathed from the ravages of the Mersey blitz.

Postwar renewal was shaped by the demand for housing, resulting in 1,500 new homes being built between 1946 and 1953. Traditional trades and industries on which Runcorn had depended for generations all but vanished in the emerging technological age. The tanneries, once centre to Britain's leather production, became victims to the growth of synthetic products. Perhaps even more symbolic, trade on the inland waterways dwindled as modern roads provided a faster transport route. However, these events pale into insignificance with the announcement in 1964 that Runcorn would be designated a 'new town' to help reduce the overcrowding problems then prevalent in Merseyside. Runcorn people took a great deal of interest in the impending changes and in 1966 almost 1 in 5 citizens visited an exhibition of designs for the new Runcorn. The Runcorn Development Corporation sought to mix old and new harmoniously, yet cleared away more of the old town and built over sixty farms and small agricultural holdings in the pastoral rural fringes of the town. The ancient village of Halton now found itself centre stage with around 7,250 acres of residential and industrial estates.

In recent times Runcorn has continued to change, so much so that the folk of two generations past would scarce believe their eyes. ICI is no longer with us, Canal Street no longer echoes to the chorus of sporting cheer and the possibility of a new Mersey crossing is once more on the horizon.

Dave Thompson

1

Bridging the River

A view of Runcorn Transporter Bridge from St Mary's church in Widnes. (*Author's Collection*)

No look at Runcorn would be complete without mention of its great river crossings. From 1178, when the charter of the ancient ferry was granted to the sixth Baron of Halton, until current times the need to cross the river has been a source of frustration for the people of Runcorn.

Above: The ancient Runcorn ferry was actually nothing more than a rowing boat, but for centuries provided the only means of crossing the river at Runcorn, short of a perilous walk over the sands or travel t Warrington. From about 1803 the ferry operated from this landing slip, seen here close to the old sal water bathhouse. Use of the ferry declined with the opening of the railway bridge and later through th disruption caused by the construction of the ship canal. The 700-year-old service closed altogether when th transporter bridge opened in 1905. (*Author's Collection*)

Below: The movement for the construction of a bridge across the Mersey was initiated at the beginning o the nineteenth century, but proposals, including one design given by Thomas Telford in 1814, came t nought until the irresistible impetus given by the railway age. The London & North Western Railway bui their crossing to provide a more direct means of rail travel between Liverpool and London. This earl photograph from 1864 shows a maze of scaffolding rising from the river as the new lattice girder iron bridg begins to take shape. (*Halton Borough Council*)

his magnificent viaduct opened in 1868 and included a tolled cantilever footway. In many ways, though, it
iled to dampen the public demand for a vehicular route to ease communication with Widnes, especially
ter the construction of the ship canal, when to use the cumbersome ferryboat passengers had to climb
ver the ship canal wall. (*Author's Collection*)

more reliable and effective means of communication needed to be found and in 1899, under the guidance of
r John Brunner, several prominent businessmen established the Runcorn & Widnes Bridge Company. The
mpany consulted with bridge engineer John Webster, who immediately recognised the technical difficulties of
ossing two busy waterways with a bridge that would not require the demolition of much of the town. Webster
commended the construction of a transporter bridge, a rare type of bridge that carried a suspended ferry above
e water, at road level, on the underside of a bridge beam which was set clear of the tallest ships. The laying of
e cylinders, which formed the foundations of the bridge in the Manchester Ship Canal, is seen here under
onstruction in 1902. (*Author's Collection*)

Construction work continues in 1903 and the 180 ft bridge towers are beginning to take shape. (*Author's Collection*)

The Arrol Bridge & Roof Company of Glasgow was the main contractor responsible for the construction of the 1,000 ft long superstructure. It was reputed that if Arrol-built bridges were placed end to end they would stretch for over 2½ miles. This photograph shows some of the Arrol workmen shortly before the bridge was completed. (*Halton Borough Council*)

Right: A portrait photograph of Sir John Brunner MP, the influential chemical manufacturer who pioneered the idea of constructing a transporter bridge at Runcorn. Brunner chaired the bridge company but even more importantly subscribed most of his own money into the share capital. Without his foresight the venture might never have occurred and many of today's readers would not be reminiscing over the old transporter bridge. (*ICI*)

Below: Sir John Brunner crosses the bridge in his own motor car. At first motor vehicles must have been a strange and exciting sight for children, so much so that local schools once had to issue warnings to children not to run after cars and charabancs as they discharged from the transporter. (*Author's Collection*)

Left: The carriage of the bridge clattered and banged to and fro across the river with journeys normally taking about three to four minutes. One of the strange quirks of the bridge in the early days was its complex charging policy. There were thirty-one separate toll charges for passengers and 112 charges in all for carrying across such commodities as cockles, vinegar, nails, oranges and pianos. It's a wonder that these passengers, who have just left the bridge at Waterloo Road, could make any sense of the charges. (*Author's Collection*)

In its early years the bridge was beset by problems. Despite its much heralded launch in front of thousands of spectators it broke down on its second day of operation and remained closed for weeks, casting doubt over the wisdom of building such a structure. Indeed, the bridge company struggled to make a profit and Sir John Brunner decided to cut his losses, selling his interests to the Widnes Corporation. They undertook major alterations to the structure before it was officially reopened in 1913. Once more Sir John Brunner performed the necessary honours. This picture shows the VIPs being whisked across the river. (*Bob Martindale*)

Throughout its fifty-six year lifespan the transporter bridge made constant news headlines. More often than not it was bad news. A steam barge crashed into a transporter tower in 1918 and over the years several vehicles drove straight off the bridge because drivers believed it was a conventional fixed bridge. This view shows a motor car being hoisted from a watery grave after the driver drove straight into the ship canal. (*Percy Dunbavand*)

Despite the frequent breaks in service, spiralling costs and lengthening queues, the transporter fell victim to the irresistible demands for a fixed road crossing. The bridge's days were numbered when in 1956 work commenced on a new high level road crossing. This picture captures the scenes in 1961 during the closing ceremony for the bridge. During its last trip crowds thronged the streets to witness the specially pre-selected passengers depart for Widnes. In a ceremony that would have befitted the launch of a great ship, flags were hoisted, Runcorn parish church rang out a peal of bells and ships' sirens sounded as the transporter car slipped away for the last time. (*Author's Collection*)

This unique meeting took place during the closing ceremony of the transporter bridge. On the left is 84-year-old Mr Shaw, the first driver of the transporter during its opening in 1905, and on the right Mr Done, the last driver of the transporter carriage during the closing ceremony. (*Halton Borough Council*)

The construction of the new road bridge blighted those parts of old Runcorn unfortunate enough to be in the line of its approaches. It resulted in the demolition of many old Victorian terraces and familiar landmarks like Abel's boat yard, which is seen here amid the construction site. (*Jim Polding*)

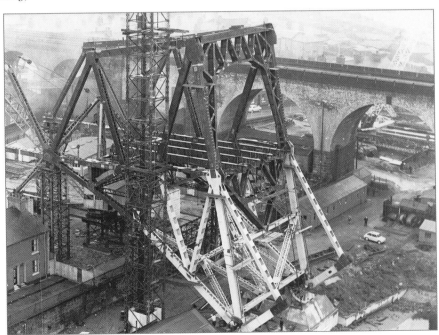

Onwards and upwards, the massive steel structure begins to rise over surrounding streets; it would soon dominate the skyline. (*Halton Borough Council*)

The rising arch extends slowly away from the Runcorn shoreline. On the top of the structure is the 20-ton creeper crane which held the steelwork in place while riveters assembled the massive 1,628 ft span. (*Halton Borough Council*)

The bridge works required more than 2 miles of approach road to be prepared across old Runcorn. As evident in this 1959 picture this required the excavation of large amounts of soap waste on the east side of Greenway Road – a brief reminder that soap manufacture was one of Runcorn's pioneering industries in the early years of the nineteenth century. Interestingly, bridge excavation work near to this site in 1960 revealed 200-year-old wooden water pipes. (*Halton Borough Council*)

The bridge assembly works in June 1960. When completed the bridge would become the third largest steel arch span in the world, only surpassed in size by the Sydney Harbour Bridge and Bayonne Bridge at New York. (*Arthur Orchard*)

A unique view of Runcorn from the massive steel structure. (*Halton Borough Council*)

Bridge 'spiderman' and other steelworkers enjoy a well-earned tea break after scaling the heights of the soaring arch. On the right is steel erector Terry Burns. On 6 November 1960 he guided the last girder in place before jumping the narrow gap between the two 280 ft high halves of the span. His daring leap claimed all the headlines in the following day's press. (*Terry Burns*)

This view from the Old Quay locks shows the first complete view of all three Mersey crossings at Runcorn creating for a short while prior to the demolition of the transporter bridge probably the only place in the world where three bridges crossed a 1,000 ft span in such proximity. (*Author's Collection*)

2

Chapels & Churches

Bob Hulse leads the choir procession into Runcorn parish church. (*Mildred Walker*)

'Runcorn, where we see nothing but a fair parish church,
a parsonage, and a few scattered tenements.'
Daniel King, *The Vale Royal of England*, 1656

Above: An etching of the medieval parish church a Runcorn. This church was close to the site of the first church which Princess Ethelfleda established soon after Runcorn was founded in 915. Several generations of the Brooke family, including Sir Richard Brooke, the founder of the family dynasty who first leased Norton Priory from the crown, were buried here. The Norman building fell into a deplorable state of disrepair in the early nineteenth century and was finally demolished in 1846, prior to being replaced by a stunning new church building. (*Author's Collection*)

Left: The new Runcorn parish church looked resplendent and was designed by architect Anthon Salvin with a magnificent 161ft steeple. Like the medieval church before, this church continued to remain the focus for much of Runcorn's spiritual life until other faiths and denominations establishe a firmer presence. (*Author's Collection*)

side the building marble and stained glass commemorate the lives of those who have brought credit and rvice to the town, including fresh generations of the Brooke family. There are windows dedicated to rincess Ethelfleda and James Wilding, the eminent local surveyor who was responsible the construction of any of Runcorn's best-known buildings. (*Author's Collection*)

. rare view of the bell ringers at Runcorn parish church posing alongside one of the ancient bells from the hurch. The ancient church had a peal of five bells, four of which had been taken for hanging in the new church esigned by Salvin. The remaining bell, dating from 1628, went to Holy Trinity church. (*Mildred Walker*)

Amid great spectacle the choir processes from the church. In the background the transporter bridge can be clearly seen. (*Author's Collection*)

The vicar of Runcorn, George Davidson, pictured with the church choir in the 1950s. (*Mildred Walker*)

Methodism took a strong hold in Runcorn to the extent that it was once thought there were as many Methodists as Anglicans. Nothing illustrates the growth and significance of Methodism more than the grandeur of St Paul's Methodist church. This marvellous building was built in 1866 and graced High Street until its demolition in 1969. (*Author's Collection*)

...e magnificent ...ditorium of St Paul's ...s known for its fine ...oustics and organ. ...ring the war the ...urch became a ...pular venue for ...ncerts. The church ...o contained a ...emorial to Thomas ...zelhurst, the local ...ap manufacturer ...d Methodist bene- ...ctor who generously ...ded the construc- ...n of most Methodist ...apels in Runcorn. (*...uthor's Collection*)

The church of St Michael and All Angels was built to serve the rapidly expanding population around Greenway Road. Indeed, so essential was the church that for years an impatient congregation held services in the partially completed building. The architect's original plans included a steeple but this was never built. St Michael's gained a new dignity in 1931 when it became a parish church, independent of Runcorn parish church. (*Author's Collection*)

...ncorn Spiritualist church is one of Runcorn's ...ost novel churches, nestling underneath the ...lway bridge arches at Ashridge Street. The ...urch was originally built by the Primitive ...ethodists as an offshoot of the Greenway Road ...apel to help mission the Dukesfield area. This ...w shows the rear of the church from Brackley ...eet. (*Dave Thompson*)

Above: Welsh Chapel at Waterloo Road was built in 1856 and recalls a time when Runcorn had a sizeable trade with the North Wales coast. The little brick-built building only ceased being a place of worship in recent years and was the oldest nonconformist chapel still in use until that time. Welsh Chapel managed to escape likely demolition when the road bridge approaches were built, only to fall victim to a dwindling congregation. (*Dave Thompson*)

Left: Runcorn has seen a plethora of churches come and go in the last two centuries but one of the more fascinating to have endured is Christ Church at Weston Point Docks. The magnificent little church on the island was built in 1841 by the Trustees of the Weaver Navigation to provide their workers with a ready means of worship. One strange feature of the building is that a century passed before a marriage ceremony was undertaken. It closed in 1993 but has managed to survive risk of demolition. Fortunately this charming little church is now a listed building. (*Dave Thompson*)

3

The Streets of Our Town

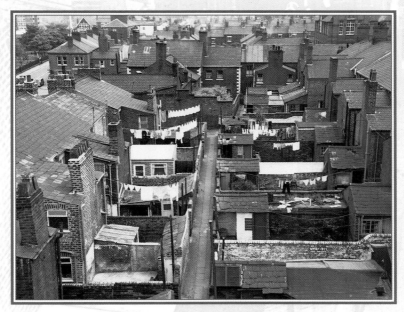

The back alleyways of Speakman Street and Grove Street. (*Roy Gough*)

'A meager, uninteresting, shabby brick town with irregular streets,
looking like a dwarfed, stunted city.'
Nathaniel Hawthorne, *Our Old Home*, 1863

This town centre view reveals the old and the new in the 1960s. The Bethesda church and St Pau
overshadow the new market place and bus station. Old Runcorn was once well known for its friend
gossipy shopping thoroughfares, narrow streets and well-stocked shops. (*Roy Gough*)

The top of Bridge Street showing many of the shops which are no longer with us. On the left in this 197
picture is Riley's TV shop and on the right are Littlemores and Charlie Manning's newsagents. (*Roy Gough*)

e transporter bridge forms a marvellous backdrop to the lower part of Bridge Street. On the right is the
d market place. (*Roy Gough*)

re is another view of the market place. In the background is Handley & Becks. (*Roy Gough*)

The view down Ellesmere Street from the old market place. The pub on the corner is the Commercial Hotel or 'Glass Barrel' as it was best known. This pub actually had several names over the years but only one celebrity landlord. The famous Widnes rugby star Tommy McCue was pulling the pints here in the late 1950s. (*Roy Gough*)

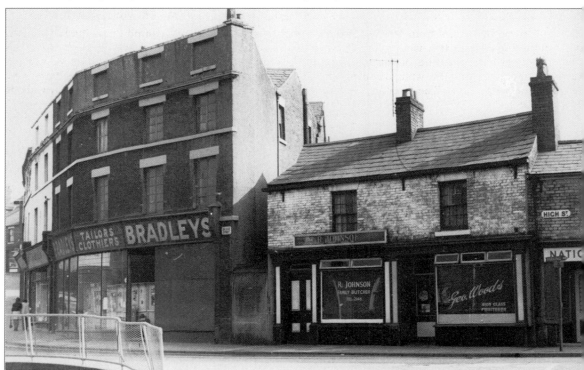

bove: This marvellous view from 1905 provides another glimpse of the area around the old police station. n interesting feature in this view is the fountain which once provided Runcorn with a ready source of esh water until the opening of the reservoir on Runcorn Hill. So many people continued using it fterwards that in 1894 the water supply was stopped because the fountain was alleged to have been amaging the water rate. The fountain was later converted to a gas lamp standard and removed about 948. (*Author's Collection*)

Opposite: Bradley's tailor's shop and Johnson's the butcher's lodged in between Bridge Street and High Street. Almost out of view on the right are the National Coal Board offices where local people paid for their coal deliveries. (*Roy Gough*)

The changing face of Bridge Street in the 1970s. Much of the Ellesmere Street estate was cleared for a new housing development. (*Roy Gough*)

A view of Regent Street in the early 1970s. Most shops seen here have also disappeared over the past thirty years. Readers may recall Ron Prince's butcher's shop, barber Charlie Nixon and Blundell's. (*Roy Gough*)

A panoramic view over Church Street, 1995. (*Dave Thompson*)

A view along Church Street, early 1970s. Well-known shops of yesteryear include Hamlett's butcher's shop, Ducketts' fish and veg shop, Lea's ironmonger's, Calvert's tailor's, Melias' grocery shop, and Dawson's music shop. (*Roy Gough*)

A view along Church Street, looking towards Runcorn Parish School and McDermott's chemist's, ear
1970s. The 150-year-old school building was demolished in 1976, losing one of the best-known features
the area. (*Roy Gough*)

Devonshire Square was once a busy and popular centre in the old town. Among other things the squa
used to be the main platform for hustings at election time and many an evangelical crusade was launche
in the cobbled thoroughfare. The Salvation Army held an open-air service for many years in front of th
Masonic Hotel. (*Author's Collection*)

osville's Castlefields service passes through High Street. Braverman's antique shop and the New Inn pub
n be seem in the background. Out of view on the opposite side of the road is the Scala – the old picture
use once famed for its westerns. The Scala showed its last film in 1957, and is now a popular bingo hall.
oy Gough)

*i*other view of the High Street in the 1970s. This shows the Midland Bank and Manweb showrooms.
oy Gough)

As we have seen, many of the streets of our town have undergone a great deal of change; others, like Albert Street, have disappeared altogether. The pub on the corner is the London and North Western, a favourite watering hole for Empress Cinema goers after a night at the flicks. (*Roy Gough*)

Lowlands Road was once a busy district in the town with old-fashioned end of terrace shops, but little now remains of the area. (*Roy Gough*)

The view down Waterloo Road. The Queens is one of the dozens of pubs to have disappeared from Runcorn over the last century. In 1906 Runcorn had ninety-seven beer sellers and licensed premises. Astonishingly, that was one licensee for every 217 inhabitants of the town. (*Roy Gough*)

A panoramic view from the transporter bridge showing the terraced streets in the district around the South Bank pub. Before 1876 the pub was the home of the prominent local shipbuilder Dennis Brundrit, and many of the folk in the surrounding streets doubtless worked at his waterfront boat yard. This area was once quite vibrant with plenty of shops along Lord Street, Ashridge Street and Rutland Street. (*Jim Polding*)

This picture from the tower of the transporter bridge shows the other end of Waterloo Road. It provides good view of the churchyard, still with the gravestones standing upright prior to their being laid down 1963. The oldest stone in the ancient burial ground dates from 1626. (*Jim Polding*)

Opposite: A view of the old white-washed quarrymen's cottages at Runcorn Hill. The terraced row Highlands Road was earlier known as 'Snuffy Row', a reference to the fact that many of the occupants we well known for their use of snuff. This particular view from the early 1900s shows Highlands Road nothing more than a rough track over the quarry spoil. (*Betty Helsby*)

pony and trap pass along Moughland Lane. In 1944 this lane had the distinction of being the first
adway to be relit with street lighting after years of wartime blackout conditions. (*Author's Collection*)

On the opposite side of Runcorn Hill is Weston Road. This is one of the oldest and best-known roads in t district which links Runcorn and Weston village. (*Percy Dunbavand*)

Runcorn Heath in the early 1900s, shortly after it was landscaped as a park complete with lake a children's playground. The track to the left is Park Road. The view shows open fields as far as Halton Cast (*Author's Collection*)

4

People's Century

A picture of Camden Methodist Sunday school from 1968. More than a century
of celebration, events and praise has been captured in the hands of local people.
The emergence of the camera has made it possible for us to glimpse
what happened before us. (*Roy Gough*)

Without doubt the highlight of Runcorn's social year was the annual Whitsuntide walks through the tow
The origins are not known but they had become a local institution by 1909 when this picture was take
The various Sunday school walks amalgamated over time, joining together the processions of the Fr
churches, Catholics and Anglicans along one annual route. Civic notables, friendly societies and tra
associations also joined in the fun but were not part of the main procession. (*Betty Helsby*)

Once again the silken banners make an appearance in another flamboyant and proud display
of commitment to the Sunday schools. This is the 1926 Whit Walk passing along High Street.
(*John Cook*)

year later and All Saints' Mission are seen participating in the 1927 Whit Monday procession. (*Betty
lsby*)

the name on the banner suggests, in this
51 Whit Monday procession Mill Brow
ission once supported the very poorest
ildren; it was an outrider to Holy Trinity.
er 4,000 people took part in the 1951
ocession, including James Richardson of
oughland Lane, then attending his 77th
nual Whit Walk in Runcorn. (*John Cook*)

The Whit Monday procession in 1948 involved 3,000 walkers, demonstrating the commitment of t townsfolk to reviving their traditions after years when the war had made the walks impossib A Sunday school, representing either the Anglican, Catholic or Free churches, took it in turns every year

...ad the procession. This year it was the turn of St Edward's, representing the Roman Catholic Church, ...llowed by the Runcorn Silver Band. This view of the procession shows the walkers making their way ...rough Devonshire Square. (*John Cook*)

Although there was the occasional change, processions invariably made their way up Greenway Road, where they ended at a service on Runcorn Heath. The Heath Methodist church is seen in the foreground of this picture en route to Runcorn Heath, where in the latter years of the Whit tradition a fairground was also held. (*Roy Gough*)

The Heath Methodist church assembles on Runcorn Heath. The church was created in 1970 from the congregations of four older Methodist chapels in Runcorn. Soon afterwards the tradition of Whit walking all but disappeared. (*Roy Gough*)

Today it is hard to imagine how important the annual Whit Walks, parades and carnivals of yesteryear were to people. These events offered an opportunity to display regalia and banners and dress in costumes. This marvellous picture from 1909 shows two Runcorn children revealing how their own grandparents might well have looked in times past. (*Margaret Marsh*)

Above: This picture was taken at Billy Moore's yard c
Norfolk Street and shows the local Oddfellows lodg
known as Rose of Sharon, preparing to join th
procession through the town. The United Order c
Oddfellows had a few local branches, of which th
Rose of Sharon was the largest. (*Margaret Marsh*)

Left: For many years the UNA Carnival was also a we
supported tradition. A parade went through the tow
and the festive glory was saved for Canal Street whe
the crowning ceremony of the Carnival Queen wa
held. This Carnival Queen from the early 1930s
Amy Wilson. (*Betty Helsby*)

modern times the Town Park Show became something of a tradition, attracting large numbers of people,
arity stalls and entertainers. However, this Family Funday in Runcorn's largest park, seen here in 1995,
appeared from the social calendar in 2000. (*Dave Thompson*)

e uniformed youth services have always been well supported in Runcorn. This is an outing of the 5th
ncorn Guides at Frodsham Hill in 1937. (*May Martin*)

The 5th Runcorn Brownies assemble in the vicarage grounds in Highlands Road, *c.* 1937. (*May Martin*)

The Guides and Brownies come together for a parade at Runcorn Football Club's Canal Street ground (*May Martin*)

The scouting movement began in Runcorn with the formation of the 1st Weston & Weston Point Scouts in 1908, less than twelve months after Baden Powell had founded the organisation. Over the years there have been ten local groups, of which the 4th Runcorn Scouts is one of the largest. They were formed at Bold Street in 1923 and moved to Runcorn Heath in 1953, where they still operate from their scout hut. This picture was taken on Runcorn Heath in 1963 and shows the leading competitors for the swimming cup. (*John Frodsham*)

Children from the Mill Brow Mission enjoy a summer outing in 1938. (*John Cook*)

Waiting for the coach to arrive at Brunswick Hall. The Cooper Street Mission assembles for their summer trip to New Brighton. Cooper Street was another one of those thriving communities that has long since disappeared. (*Betty Helsby*)

nateur dramatic societies also played an important role in the cultural life of the town, especially before evision grabbed the attention of viewers. This picture shows members of the Holy Trinity Amateur amatic Society at a dress rehearsal for another sell-out play. (*Margaret Marsh*)

the world's a stage: another scene being performed by the Holy Trinity Amateur Dramatic Society. Other ll-known amateur dramatic groups then active in the town included those at Camden Methodists and the Johns Presbyterian Amateur Dramatic Society. (*Margaret Marsh*)

Runcorn's Highfield Male Voice Choir was founded in 1911, providing a rewarding outlet for many a aspiring young chorister, while at the same time, offering first-class entertainment. The first conce performance was given at the Widnes Eisteddfod, where they won first prize. Over the decades the choir h continued to flourish and has played in leading venues, including the Royal Albert Hall. This 1992 view the choir shows another trophy that was won for their choral talents. (*Highfield MVC*)

Venues for public entertainment have come and gone. One of the best remembered is the 1,088-se Empress Cinema on Lowlands Road. During its fifty-year history the Empress covered the period from sile films to the epic Hollywood blockbusters, time in which people's leisure interests have changed dramatica The last film shown at the Empress in June 1973 was Stanley Kubrick's *Clockwork Orange*. (*Roy Gough*)

ncorn folk enjoyed their outdoor entertainment. This scene from 1958 shows the old bandstand at ncorn Hill. It used to be a favourite venue for the Runcorn Pioneer Band, and many visiting bands from ross Cheshire. The bandstand once attracted large crowds for a Sunday afternoon concert. (*Edna Lea*)

chdeacon Alfred Maitland Wood (standing far left) is pictured in 1912 at his private garden party in the arage grounds at Highlands Road. His guests enjoyed an afternoon of tea, fresh cakes and croquet on the arage lawn. (*Betty Helsby*)

It is often overlooked that Runcorn is the birthplace of one of the great novelists of the Victorian era. Although his association with the town was a fleeting one, Sir Thomas Hall Caine was born at Bridgewater Street in 1853. An author and playwright of some renown, his books sold in their millions, and he particularly found fame in the Isle of Man where he lived most of his life. Hall Caine was a close friend of Dracula author Bram Stoker and spent some time as secretary to Dante Gabriel Rossetti. Later in life he commented that he wished to visit his humble birthplace, but never made time. The author's only impression of Runcorn came when he passed over the railway bridge en route to Liverpool. (*Manx National Heritage*)

5

Waterways at Work

Anderton Canal Carrying Co. narrow boats tied up at Top Locks. (*Author's Collection*)

'Upon the river which washes the shore of the town innumerable craft
spread their sails, and, beating time to the ceaseless murmur of the waters,
are heard the whirr of wheels, the rattle of machinery,
and the loud hum of commerce.'
Charles Nickson, *History of Runcorn*, 1887

The Bridgewater Canal is distinguished as one of England's pioneering canals, and its development mark[s] the beginnings of Runcorn's prominence for waterways. This 1970s view shows the widest part of the can[al] at Top Locks, an area which once thronged with boats waiting to descend the locks beyond Waterloo Brid[ge] However, it was not always possible for boatmen to ply their trade and they endured periods of hardsh[ip] when the canals were frozen and boats were left stranded. It is even on record that in one of the fier[ce] winters of the 1890s horses and traps could cross the canal at this point. (*Roy Gough*)

Two lines of ten locks formed the Runcorn terminus of the Bridgewater Canal. This scene from 1929 sho[ws] the view looking down the old line of locks towards Bridgewater House. The old line closed in 1939 becau[se] of the decline in the use of the canal, and the locks were filled in ten years later. The second line of loc[ks] often referred to as the new line, was lost in 1966. (*Author's Collection*)

rare view from about 1906 showing the busy bottom locks. Just in view on the left is the old Customs
use, built in the 1860s. (*Percy Dunbavand*)

seems hard to imagine that this scene was the same one which many years earlier bustled with narrow
ats and barges. The background is Hankey Street and the back of Rutland Street. (*Roy Gough*)

The old tonnage office near Crescent Row is pictured here in 1969 prior to its demolition. The canalside office was where records were once kept of the cargo of craft passing through the locks. (*Roy Gough*)

In this scene from 1970 narrow boats pass by the Navigation Inn at Canal Street. This old watering hole was once a calling-in point for Captain Edward Smith of the *Titanic*. In his early years, before taking command of the world's most famous passenger liner, Captain Smith used to travel down the canal on his brother's narrowboat. He became good friends with the landlord. (*Roy Gough*)

other canalside scene alongside the Camden Tannery. Already evident in this scene from the late 1960s
hat pleasure craft had become the main users of the canal. Even the narrow boat shown here has a cargo
people. (*Roy Gough*)

o narrow boats pass the demolished tannery site in 1969. This area is now the site of the Brindley Arts
tre. (*Roy Gough*)

The Big Pool in 1923 with the Simpson and Davies boat yard to the left. This local firm was founded about 1860 and operated a large fleet of narrow boats on the canal. They were also colliery agen supplying slack and coal to local industry. (*Author's Collection*)

The passing of the town's importance inland waterway traffic is told in thi picture of Big Pool In what remains o the basin the mouldering hulks sunken barges can be seen. Records show this area wa once the graveyar for forty-one barge four lighters, three caissons and twen two mud boats. (*Roy Gough*)

s intriguing 1969 view of the Bridgewater Canal at Preston Brook shows the rural scene around the area
he Marina. These fields are now covered by many hundreds of houses, stretching as far as Norton Water
ver. (*Roy Gough*)

Manchester Ship
al opened in 1894,
viding Runcorn with
eep-water artery to
nchester and
tham, although at the
of losing its
rfront. The ship canal
a momentous
ineering feat, taking
years to complete and
ploying 16,000
vies. It swelled the
ulation of the town
waterborne trade
rished. One
temporary account
cribed it as 'one of the
ld's great victories of
noblest sort'. This
w shows construction
er way near Castle
k. (*Author's Collection*)

Runcorn's shore posed engineers with one of the most difficult stretches of the 34-mile ship canal. A gan
wall was built to separate the old Mersey waterfront with the river, and further excavations of the sto
promontory near Castle Rock were required. (*Halton Borough Council*)

ht: Runcorn once had a
utation, stretching back as far as
early eighteenth century, for
structing small river craft.
eral boat-building yards were
ablished on the Mersey shore at
stle Rock, Belvedere and Old
ay. One of the best known was
hard Abel's boat yard, seen here
Castle Rock. Abel's was founded
1869, and the family firm also
rated wharfs at Liverpool,
kenhead and a repair yard at
ston Point Docks. The last
oden barge built on the Mersey
Runcorn was launched from here
1953. (*Bill Leathwood*)

Left: A 1929 view of the canalfront at
the Old Quay boat yard. The yard was
established in about 1804 for the
opening of the Runcorn to Latchford
Canal. Its prominence grew considerably
when the ship canal was constructed and
the yard served as the repair yard for the
Manchester Ship Canal Company's
floating craft. (*Author's Collection*)

ht: The Hong Kong-registered
llaman passes Old Quay boat
d in 1994. At its height 280
f worked at the old boat yard,
luding shipwright's joiners,
ermakers and platers. Sadly,
yard closed in 2003 after
ost two centuries of service
keeping the local waterways
good order.
ve Thompson)

Above: A ship passes under the transporter bridge in 1959. (*Denis Hamilton*)
Below: This magnificent three-masted schooner berthed in front of Bridgewater House in 1973 and attract
many visitors keen to recall the old days of sail when schooners were a common sight on the ship can
This particular topsail schooner was originally called *Eva* and traded in Scandinavian waters as the *Mo*
Jan. However, the ship is best remembered as *Charlotte Rhodes* in the BBC drama *The Onedin Line*. (*Roy Goug*

sixteen years the
randa Guinness sailed
tween the Guinness
ewery at Dublin and
ncorn. The 1,540-ton
sel was built in 1976
d was the world's first
rpose-built beer tanker;
e could hold
370,000 pints of
inness. The *Miranda
inness* is pictured here
1993 on a final visit to
Wigg Island berth.
ncorn Weekly News)

nodern view of shipping on the ship canal. The 'Arklow' vessels are a group of Irish-based bulk carriers
ich still regularly pass through Runcorn en route to Manchester. (*Dave Thompson*)

A scene at Runcorn docks more than a century ago. Large quantities of china clay, china stone and feldsp
arrived here destined for the Potteries. Coal, salt and chemicals were other prime types of cargo for ships
the port. By 1885 the docks were handling 500,000 tons a year, equivalent to 100 vessels a day. T
prosperity of the docks slumped after the First World War but fortunes were revived after the opening
Runcorn Bridge. (*Author's Collection*)

The cargoes may have changed but this modern view from 1995 shows that many foreign vessels are s
visiting Runcorn docks. (*Dave Thompson*)

ayside scene at Runcorn Docks. A crane is discharging the cargo from the *Volente*. (*Author's Collection*)

s scene shows china clay being discharged from the 631-ton SS *Moelfre Rose* into the Alfred Dock sheds.
 coaster was built in 1921 and was a regular visitor to local docks. (*Author's Collection*)

Quaysides were a hive of activity. Here we see crushed china stone being moved on the quay at Flint Wh
(*Author's Collection*)

A similar scene at Weston Point Docks. Castner Kellner can be seen in the background. (*Author's Collectio*

6

All Our Working Lives

The waterways, chemical works, quarries and other industries from Runcorn's past gave rise to a plethora of trades and professions. Many of them are no longer with us. This shows the Castner Kellner firefighters with the shield they won in 1908. *(ICI)*

A view of rural Weston Point in 1892 before the Castner Kellner factory cast a permanent shadow over future of the area. Within a few years large areas of this idyllic spot overlooking the river would becom hive of industrial development. (*ICI*)

An early view of the Castner Kellner works shortly after the factory opened in 1897. The factory was built the Aluminium Company of Oldbury, in the Black Country, who were attracted here by the ready workfo and Runcorn's location close to the Cheshire salt fields. The company were also doubtless impressed by ease with which raw materials could be transported on the new Manchester Ship Canal. (*ICI*)

astner Kellner's first electrolytic plant in the course of construction. This was the largest plant of its kind in e world for the electrolytic decomposition of brine. In 1927 experienced workers from Oldbury were cruited to operate the plant, swelling the Weston Point workforce to 1,000. (*ICI*)

aces from the past. Women workers at Castner Kellner, *c.* 1916. Women played an important role keeping 1e wheels of industry turning during the First World War, and undertook many traditionally male-ominated roles in the local chemical works and tanneries. Among other things they helped manufacture roducts used in the production of high explosives and mustard gas. Many Runcorn women also travelled to ork at factories in Widnes or at Helsby wire works. (*Dave Thompson*)

Castner Kellner, and the other chemical works later built at Rocksavage and Wigg Island, became t
mainstay of employment for generations of Runcornians. Many thousands of local people have worked at
factories in Runcorn, many giving their entire working lives to the service of the company. This view sho
John Thompson on his retirement from the company in 1953. It followed forty-two years' service at Castr
Kellner. (*Dave Thompson*)

Right: Salt Union was founded
in 1888 and established works
at Weston Point. However, the
company only really expanded
when the construction of the
ship canal provided it with this
deep-water wharf from which
salt could be exported. A
vacuum plant was later built
in 1911, vastly expanding
production and making Salt
Union one of the largest salt
producers in the world.
(*Salt Union*)

gg Island was another industrial area that expanded rapidly because the ship canal afforded it a deep-
ter wharf. This view of the works was taken in about 1900. (*ICI*)

1937 there was large expansion of industrial development at Wigg Island when ICI was given permission
secretly build a shadow factory for the production of chemical weapons. The Randle works operated in
nplete secrecy and during the war Runcorn folk came to know it as the 'hush hush works'. This is a rare
w inside Wigg Works East taken in 1928. (*ICI*)

The Sprinch boat yard on the Bridgewater Canal was one of the best boat yards in the country, with some the finest craftsmen and facilities. Opened in 1890 to serve the Bridgewater Canal, and later managed by t Manchester Ship Canal Company, the dockyard was at one time responsible for the servicing a maintenance of over 250 craft. Sprinch closed as a boat yard in 1948. (*Percy Dunbavand*)

Quarrying was one of Runcorn's oldest industries and its heyday came in the nineteenth century when t great port of Liverpool could not get enough of either Runcorn or Weston sandstone. This is a view of t Runcorn Hill quarries in 1887. The hill was one of the largest and most successful quarries, as were tho nearby at Weston. Smaller quarries operated at both Mill Brow and Stenhills. (*Author's Collection*)

ove: A view of the South Quarry at Weston taken about
98. This quarry, sometimes called the Rockfield or
me's Quarry, provided massive blocks of the finest stone
use in public works at Liverpool and elsewhere. At full
duction as many as 700 men worked the Weston
arries and immigrant workers came to settle here from
rth Wales and Cumbria. (*Author's Collection*)

ht: Stone was exported from both the Runcorn Hill and
ston quarries by the use of railway lines under Weston
ad. The blocks were transported down to the docks at
ston Port from where they could be exported by boat to
final destination. (*Author's Collection*)

Runcorn and Weston stone was of a rich pink or red colour and immensely popular with architects because
was free of pebbles, durable and finely textured. It can be found in many of the region's finest buildings and w
also exported. Peel Castle in the Isle of Man, Holker Hall in Cumbria and Perch Fort Rock at New Brighton a
among the buildings built with large quantities of Runcorn stone. This view shows Weston quarryman Dav
Kinsey posing alongside a 9-ton block of stone destined for use at Liverpool Cathedral. (*Author's Collection*)

Today there is nothing to remind us that a century ago Runcorn was the most important centre for tanni
in Britain, owing largely to the ease by which hides, bark, twigs and chromium compounds could
transported by our local waterways. This view shows the Highfield tannery shortly after its closure in 196
The yard once produced all classes of leather including shoe soles and fine upholstery. At its peak Highfi
processed 8,000 hides per week. Tanning was a long and toilsome process and it once took four years
process the 3 cwt skin of a dead hippopotamus from Manchester Zoo! (*Roy Gough*)

uritan Tannery at Halton Road was founded during the First World War and built on the site of an earlier
nnery. It was taken over by Henry Boston, and its heyday came under his management. At one time
uritan employed around 300 people, and produced 7,000,000 pounds of leather a year. Posters for Puritan
ather were a common sight on hoardings across the country and helped introduce the name of the
uncorn firm to consumers nationwide. (*Catalyst Museum*)

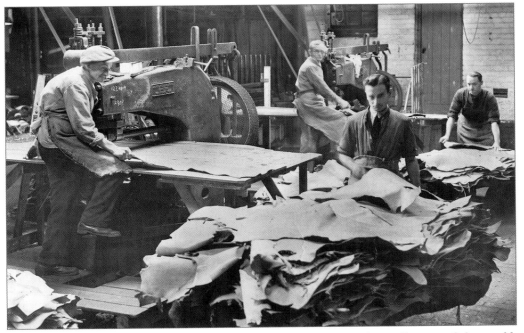

A scene inside a Runcorn tannery. Hides came to the tanneries from all parts of the world,
including South America, Nigeria, East Africa and Australia. The four largest and best known
tanneries were Highfield, Camden, Astmoor and Puritan. (*Catalyst Museum*)

The works of the Evans Sons, Lescher & Webb Biological Institute at Penn Lane developed a worldwide reputation for the manufacture of anti-toxins, sera and vaccines. The Evans' laboratories particular contribution was to aid Britain's drug supply during two world wars. This picture shows the serum laboratory where Evans developed tetanus and other vaccines. The works continued to expand in the coming decades but closed in 1981. (*Harry Thompson*)

The presence of several important waterways saw many maritime trades flourish in old Runcorn. The town had several sail makers and one of these trades to this day. The sail-making firm Robert Grieg's was established in 1923 using the loft here at the Bridgewater Stables near Waterloo Bridge. The company managed to survive the decline of the waterways and following the demolition of their premises in 1975 continued to operate from Irwell Lane. The family-run business is now one of Runcorn's oldest firms. (*Roy Gough*)

7

Making the News

Princess Margaret visited Victoria Road School in 1986, shortly after a campaign
had successfully been mounted to prevent the school's closure. This is just one of the
many hundreds of news events that fed the presses of the town's newspapers.
(*Runcorn Weekly News*)

Inset, right: No event captured public interest more than the First World War. Almost one in five Runcorn men answered Lord Kitchener's call to arms, of which 400 lost their lives at the front. Every twist and turn in the conflict was analysed in the columns of the *Weekly News* and special mention was given to the individual fortunes of local men. Among them one particular Runcorn soldier made headlines when in 1916 he was awarded the Victoria Cross. Pte Thomas 'Todger' Jones charged

Left: When Pte 'Todger' Jones, from the Cheshire Regiment, returned home for two weeks' leave in 1916 the ecstatic reception he received made front-page headlines in the national press. Thousands of people thronged the streets to welcome home the town's war hero, and Jones could hardly make it to his Princess Street home. At his VC investiture at Buckingham Palace the king marvelled at his daring heroics and reputedly enquired, 'How the dickens did you do it, Jones?' Todger's heroism did not end there: a year later he won the Distinguished Conduct Medal for more battlefront heroics, this time for repeatedly charging across the battlefield to deliver messages while under incessant fire. (*Mildred Walker*)

...oss the Somme battlefield and single-handedly ...ptured over one hundred German troops from ...emy trenches, while being fired upon repeatedly and ...en receiving bullet holes through his helmet and ...thing. (*Mildred Walker*)

Left: In 1988 the 22nd Cheshire Regiment received the Freedom of th Borough of Halton, and as can be se in this picture troops paraded throug the centre of town to mark the occasion. The old county regiment h a long occasion with the town. Duri the First World War large numbers c men from the town's works joined th regiment. The Runcorn Home Guard was also attached to the regiment fr 1940. (*Alan Roberts*)

Below: Labour schemes during the depression of the 1920s ensured tha the town's long-term unemployed w put to work, creating new parks and roads in Runcorn. The Mill Brow Quarry at Sewell Street was first to b transformed, making Rock Park in 1921. The following year it was the turn of the old Runcorn Hill quarrie and 280 men set to work to transfor it into a park. This view from 1922 shows the stone concert platform an footpaths created under the labour scheme. (*Author's Collection*)

[ab]ove: The visit in 1925 of King George V
[ca]used considerable excitement in
[Ru]ncorn. The king's every move, from his
[arr]ival on the transporter bridge to his
[de]parture from the fringes of the town,
[wa]s watched by joyful crowds. He is seen
[her]e climbing the steps of the transporter
[bri]dge's car after he asked to take a closer
[loo]k at the way the bridge operated.
(*[Au]thor's Collection*)

[Rig]ht: In 1937 Runcorn brought out the
[bu]nting once again and hoisted the flags
[to c]elebrate the coronation of King George V.
[Th]is rare picture shows a gathering of
[chi]ldren in Heath Road. (*Harry Thompson*)

Above: Runcorn had a proud tradition the voluntary uniformed services playing an active role in the life of the town. Among these is the Runcorn Sea Scouts. They were formed in 1925 by Commander W. L. Rossiter RNR and was 130-strong within twelve month, twice the size of the Wimbledon corps which at that time was regarded as the elite of the movement. This picture of the Runcorn Sea Scouts was taken in about 1939. (*Christine McGugan*)

Left: Airline pilot Eric Robinson made news headlines in 1938 when he tw flew Prime Minister Neville Chamberlain to Germany for meeting with Adolf Hitler. The Runcornian, once heralded as 'Britain's most experienced airman', was the pilot of the plane when Chamberlain returned promising 'peace in our time.' Robinson made headlines again only weeks afterwards when he was killed in an air crash at Portishead, Somerset. (*June Carrington*)

ve: In 1942 Runcorn adopted the sloop HMS
ningo. Thereafter the townsfolk paid great attention
he adventures of the ship throughout the
nainder of the war. The Council sent the crew
ristmas gifts and many young people in Runcorn
iblished pen pals on board ship. (*Author's Collection*)

ht: In June 1945 a contingent from the ship's
npany arrived in Runcorn. They presented a
anese flag to the town for the years of friendship
wn to the ship's crew. The flag had been
sented to HMS *Flamingo* by the army for the part
guns played in giving artillery support on the
rma coast. This picture shows Lieutenant
nmander Pounds, commanding officer of HMS
ningo, on board ship with the flag which was
sented to the chairman of Runcorn Urban
trict Council. (*Author's Collection*)

On the home front the war brought about a tremendous effort from local people. With Runcorn facing peril of invasion many people were recruited into civil defence, joining the ARP or other services. Howev in 1940 came the threat of the incendiary blitz then blighting Merseyside. The authorities began a mass recruitment campaign for fire guards and watchers. By 1942 there were 2,700 volunteers in Runco among them this detachment of fire wardens. (*Roy Gough*)

Runcorn established records for war savings that were the envy of many towns. The first war savir committee was formed in 1916, and even after the armistice carried on its work until 1946. By the end the Second World War there were still 123 savings groups and the town's total contribution had topped million. Some of this was owing to the recycling activities of committed Runcornians like these children fr Heath Road, seen here in 1942, presenting the chairman of the Council with the money they had rai from the collection of jam jars. (*Harry Thompson*)

owing D-Day in June 1945 the national press heralded the heroics of Captain Joseph Terretta and his
e Runcorn vessel the SS *Weston*. The little coaster made the most cross-channel trips on D-Day, and
ieved the quickest turn-around between the Kent coast and the Normandy beaches. This rare view
ws the SS *Weston* at Kingston Dock, Glasgow, in 1946. (*Fred Terretta*)

event made more headlines
ing the war years than VE Day.
 ending of the war saw Runcorn
icing at the news that Germany
 surrendered. This picture shows
chairman of the Urban District
ncil joining in with the party
it at Hankey Street. (*John Cook*)

In 1953 Runcorn celebrated the Queen's coronation in style, and had a few crownings of its own. Str
parties and various other festivities were held across the town. This picture shows the coronation festivi
at the Cooper Street Mission. (*Betty Helsby*)

Opposite: The Duchess of York came to Runcorn in 1991 to open the Amanda Edwards unit at Hal
Haven. Pictured with her is Dom Valdez, the founder of Halton Haven. (*Runcorn Weekly News*)

Queen and Prince Philip visited Runcorn in 1972 to officially open the new Shopping City. The precinct uded a police station, law courts, library and office blocks under an enclosed area of some 690,000 are feet. 'Shoppo', as it is still daubed, boasted of being one of the first town-centre developments under roof, but it found less favour with shoppers over time. The precinct was renamed Halton Lea in 1995. ncorn Weekly News)

In 1998 the Queen paid another visit to Runcorn. This time she came to open the Halton Partners
Centre in the former old police station at Bridge Street. Afterwards she and the Duke of Edinburgh officia
opened the Rocksavage power station. (*Runcorn Weekly News*)

8

Landmarks from the Past

The skyline of Halton pictured in 1994. The ruins of its ancient castle are one of the 176 listed buildings now being preserved in the area. However, many other landmarks have long since disappeared. (*Dave Thompson*)

Runcorn was founded in 915 by Princess Ethelfleda, the warrior daughter of Alfred the Great.
established a fortified stockade at Castle Rock for the purpose of defending the northern flank of
kingdom of Mercia against incursions by the Danes. It is not known if the stockade, romantically portra
as an idyllic castle in this century-old picture postcard, ever saw action, but the absence of Viking na
south of Runcorn implies it might well have succeeded. However, it is known that Ethelfleda's garri
provided the foundation around which the fledgling town grew. (*Author's Collection*)

Archaeological
excavations at Norton
Priory began in 1971
and revealed some of
Runcorn's earliest hist
from the time when a
house of Augustinian
canons was founded b
Four years later a
museum trust was
established. The Norto
Priory Museum Trust
buildings opened in 1
and have been attracti
visitors ever since. The
site of the medieval pr
ruins also includes a
stunning Grade 1 liste
undercroft. (*Norton Pr
Museum Trust*)

ve: Certain buildings and structures will always be linked with the Runcorn district and no landmark has
le more of an impact than Halton Castle. This view from the late 1960s shows the lofty ancient castle
s and St Mary's church at Halton surrounded by fields. The first new town houses were constructed at
ton Brook in 1967 and soon afterwards the rural setting of Halton village was lost for ever.
cy Dunbavand)

A view towards Halton Castle looking up Castle Road. A courthouse and gaol were built here in 1738,
using some of the stonework from the medieval gatehouse, first laid to waste during the Civil War. It
used as the County Assizes for the last time in 1908 and became, as is shown here, the Castle Ho
(*Author's Collection*)

The Dissolution of the Monasteries in 1536 brought religious life at Norton to an end, but in 1545
priory and its estate was bought for £1,512 by Sir Richard Brooke. The Brookes converted some of
monastic buildings into a Tudor mansion, which was replaced in about 1750 by this magnificent Georg
edifice. It was demolished in 1928, ending centuries of the Brooke family's close ties with Nort
Fortunately the ancient undercroft which had been incorporated into the mansion was saved fr
demolition and now forms part of the Norton Priory Museum Trust. (*Norton Priory Museum Trust*)

...erations of Runcorn folk knew the Old Hall at High Street. It was built in the seventeenth century and demolished in 1883 to make way for the Salvation Army's Citadel. (*Author's Collection*)

...ther Old Hall, only this one still survives at Weston village. This antique picture postcard image shows ...400-year-old building in earlier times when the medieval preaching cross was still located nearby. The ...ton Cross was later moved to a site nearer the village stores. (*Author's Collection*)

A view of Runcorn swimming baths in the early 1970s. The building was originally the town's first ma
hall built in 1856 at a cost of £1,600. Down the years the old market hall was a popular venue for dan
concerts and public meetings. (*Roy Gough*)

This appears to be a scene of rural tranquillity but is in fact the grounds of Halton Grange, the two-sto
Italianate villa built in 1856 by soap manufacturer Thomas Johnson. It later passed to tannery magr
Francis Boston and in 1932 was purchased by Runcorn Urban District Council, along with its 12-a
estate, to serve as the new town hall and grounds. The building continues to this day to be the focus
most civic occasions. Among the guests listed in the town hall visitors' book are former Prime Minis
Stanley Baldwin and Harold Wilson. (*Author's Collection*)

are view of the old cottages that once occupied Pool Hollow. This quaint area close to Halton Grange was
ooden ravine with a brook which flowed into Big Pool. (*Betty Helsby*)

gewater House was built for the Duke of Bridgewater in 1771 to serve as a rather modest residence
le he personally supervised the construction of his canal to Runcorn. One of the best known features of
building pictured here in 1994 is the false windows painted on the façade to give the impression of more
dows. (*Dave Thompson*)

With an estate of 400 acres, Halton Lodge was another key landmark. It was built for Charles Wigg, industrial magnate whose name is given to Wigg Island. However, it is perhaps best known beca generations of the Grice family lived at the lodge and many older folk still recall Grice's Farm. Halton Lo School now occupies the site of the building. (*Author's Collection*)

In the days before immunisation prevented the spread of contagious diseases it was necessary to iso sufferers from the community. The Runcorn Hill Isolation Hospital was built in 1883 at a time when town experienced outbreaks of smallpox and diphtheria. This site by the old quarries was then ru enough to isolate sufferers from the town. This view was taken in 1902, and the track is Sandy La (*Percy Dunbavand*)

...tage Hospital was built as a memorial to Queen Victoria. It opened in 1903 and was the main hospital ...the district until the opening of Halton General Hospital. It closed in the early 1980s and is now used as ...ces by the health authority. (*Author's Collection*)

...1858 the Runcorn Burial Board purchased a 13-acre site off Greenway Road to serve as the town's ...etery. The cemetery, which included this lovely old chapel, was built by T. Barry, the prominent Liverpool ...itect. He had quite an impact on the area, returning thirty years later to build St Michael's church. ...ly the two old chapels fell into disrepair and were demolished in 1995. The grave of VC hero 'Todger' ...es and two Runcorn soldiers who fought at Rorke's Drift during the Zulu Wars are nearby. ...ve Thompson)

Runcorn War Memorial was unveiled in 1920 and commemorates the 400 local men who died during
First World War. In 1948 new panels were added to commemorate the 120 war dead from the Sec
World War. (*Author's Collection*)

This Mk IV tank came to Runcorn in 1920 and was mounted on a plinth at Runcorn Heath. It
intended to be a permanent landmark to the hardship the townsfolk had endured in the First World
but was scrapped for the armaments effort when war returned in 1939. (*Percy Dunbavand*)

ncorn Waterworks opened at Runcorn Heath in 1868, providing the town with a new source of water
awn straight from a 79 ft borehole at the bottom of a 260 ft well. From here 40,000 gallons of water an
ur could be produced, although within a short space of time even this was not sufficient for industrial
ncorn's thirsty processes. This picture dates from about 1904, by which time the Heath had been laid out
the benefit of pleasure seekers. (*Author's Collection*)

though now partially masked by housing, Norton Water Tower remains one of the most famous features
the local skyline. The great tower was built in 1892 as a 672,000-gallon balancing reservoir on Liverpool
rporation's pipeline from Lake Vyrnwy. The Latin carved in the frieze at the top of the 100-ft tower
inslates as, 'This water, derived from the source of the Severn, is brought to the City of Liverpool, a
stance of 80 miles, through the mountains and over the plains of Wales and the intervening country, at
e cost of the municipality in the year of Our Lord, 1892.' The soft water provided an invaluable boost to
dustrial works in Runcorn. (*Runcorn Weekly News*)

There is no starker contrast with the other landmarks featured in this chapter than Southgate. Sir Jam
Stirling's unique design for this new town estate drew the attention of town planners from across the wor
When it opened in 1976 it was thought likely to be a model for future estates but became beset wi
problems, not least of all with its communal heating system. The colourful housing blocks and circu
windows quickly caused critics to dub it 'Legoland', an image which the estate failed to shake off. In 198
the decision was made to demolish the estate and new semi-detached houses and bungalows were built
their place. (*Runcorn Weekly News*)

9

School Days

The cast of 'Snow White and the Seven Dwarves' gather in the playground at
Parish Girls School. (*Betty Helsby*)

'Down at the school house at Runcorn,
The 'eadmaster walked in one day
Looking all 'appy and cheerful
Which wasn't his habit, they say.'

'Many Happy Returns'
from a monologue by Stanley Holloway, 1933

Schools, like much else in o[…] social history, have come an[…] gone, but one has survived[…] almost two centuries. This i[…] the façade of the old Parish[…] School building which stoo[…] on Church Street from 183[…] to 1976. Runcorn's oldest[…] school was founded in 181[…] to provide education 'for th[…] children of the poor', yet it[…] and the schools that followe[…] at Holy Trinity, Mill Brow a[…] Granville Street came to ser[…] the wider elementary needs[…] a burgeoning town. By 187[…] Runcorn had 2,199 scholar[…] (*All Saints School*)

Stern-faced pupils at the Parish School, or Runcorn National School as it was then officially known, pose[…] an early class photograph in 1881. The cost of being educated in those days was one penny a week, ris[…] to four pence as the child progressed through the various standards. (*Mildred Walker*)

e Holy Trinity Infants School was built at Pool Lane in 1839 and flourished for over a century before sing in the 1960s. For many years before its demolition in 1994 the building was used as a teacher ning centre by Cheshire County Council. (*Dave Thompson*)

lass of infants gaze awkwardly as a photographer captures the scene outside the small school in 1933. argaret Marsh)

ove: The Parish Church School underwent many alterations and extensions during its lifetime. This rare
ture shows pupils gathered during the laying of a foundation stone to mark the beginning of one
ension. (*Author's Collection*)

et: A class photograph from Victoria Road School. This school was built in 1886 and originally opened as
Greenway Road Board School for Girls but soon became a mixed school and even at one time offered
ning classes for illiterate adults. While earlier school buildings were demolished, Victoria Road School has
vived and is now the oldest school building in Runcorn. (*Margaret Marsh*)

School outings have been a long tradition with many schools, and both Chester and Liverpool have be
popular destinations. This group of Trinity School pupils in 1951 is gathered ready to see festival ships
Liverpool. (*Roy Gough*)

Memories of the Balfour Road School still endure almost thirty-five years after its closure. During the w
years the school served as one of the town's key first aid centres. (*Runcorn Weekly News*)

10

Transported Back In Time

A nostalgic look at the public and private transport of yesteryear is captured here. Earlier generations once enjoyed a slower pace of travel and with little sign of traffic jams. In a far cry from today this double-decker bus could enjoy a congestion-free journey from Widnes to Runcorn. *(Omnicolour)*

Long before the arrival of the motor car the horse and cart held sway on the highways of Runcorn. This is a photograph of the well known Weston trader Mr Mort, seen here with his fruit cart at Chapel Row – Weston Road. This picture was taken in about 1909. (*Percy Dunbavand*)

When cars finally made their appearance, only the most prominent citizens could afford to own or be chauffeured around by motor car. This view shows the vicar of Runcorn, Archdeacon Alfred Maitland Wood, ready to depart by motor car from the entrance of his Georgian vicarage at Highlands Road. (*Betty Helsby*)

Runcorn Fire Brigade with an early fire engine. Given that the vehicle travelled no faster than 15 miles per hour, let's hope the fire-fighters got to the scene in time. A voluntary fire service was first established in 1870 and became full-time in 1940 when the auxiliary fire service was formed. (*Author's Collection*)

This is the Runcorn and Widnes Co-operative Society's first bread van. The Co-op was an important organisation in Runcorn for well over a century. Their first premises opened at Devonshire Square in 1862, and after ten years the movement had 750 local members, becoming an essential aspect of daily life for shoppers. By the time of their 70th anniversary in 1932 it had grown to 16,000 local members. (*Author's Collection*)

Pictured here in 1920 is a charabanc outing of residents from Loch Street. Journeying in these open-topped vehicles with solid rubber tyres could hardly have been a pleasant experience. These days there are no residents living in Loch Street so it is difficult to imagine that it was once part of a thriving community with terraced houses either side and three different bustling pubs, the Sloop Inn, Waterman's and the Caernarfon Castle. (*Betty Helsby*)

Local industry too made good use of these newfangled motor vehicles. This was the first petrol-driven vehicle out of the Castner Kellner works at Lydiate Lane in 1915. (*ICI*)

Although this picture was taken just over thirty years ago, it has already become a delightfully nostalgic scene for it reveals the days when traffic congestion on the bridge was hardly considered. This local bus service was destined for Rhyl, then still a popular destination for holidaymakers. (*Omnicolour*)

There's a quick change of driver outside Bethesda church in High Street before the H20 service continues on its journey. The picture was taken in the early 1970s. (*Roy Gough*)

Runcorn railway station opened shortly after the great railway bridge was built over the Mersey. This vi
shows both passengers and porters looking on as a photographer captures the scene at the busy stati
Runcorn is still well served by train services, positioned as it is on the west coast mainline. (*Autho
Collection*)

A view of the Runcorn goods yard, 1960. In the background you can see the closing span of the n
Runcorn to Widnes Bridge goods yard. (*Roy Gough*)

great age of steam is captured in this 1962 view of a passenger train picking up speed as it pulls away
Runcorn station. The houses in the background are in Norman Road. (*Roy Gough*)

other 1962 view of a steam engine passing under the Heath Road bridge on its way towards Runcorn
ion. (*Roy Gough*)

Days of steam and speed. A Runcorn-bound steam locomotive hurtles across the railway bridge. This picture was taken shortly after the line's electrification in 1961. (*Roy Gough*)

Steam engines also played an important part in industrial transportation. This is the loco Castner, one of the biggest locomotives of its time. During the 1930s it handled raw materials between the Castner Kellner works and Runcorn station. (*ICI*)

11

Sporting Life

Sport has played an important part in Runcorn's social life and the fortunes of
its semi-professional football team have featured prominently since 1918.
This is the 'Linnets' treble winning team in 1980/81.
(Runcorn Weekly News)

Left: In 1891 Sam Houghton became the first Runcornian to play international rugby for England. In the years ahead several other Runcorn players, including Albert Fildes, also received international caps. Th rare picture from about 1930 shows the England and St Hel rugby star meeting school boy at the Parish Church Boys' School. Fildes was himself an ' boy' of the parish. (*Betty Helsb*

Right: The local tanneries had a strong sporting tradition, which was supported by the tannery owners. This is the Astmoor tannery football team in 1922–23. (*Author's Collection*)
Below: The Runcorn FC team pose with the Cheshire Senior Cup after their 1936 triumph over Maccles-field. The 1930s was great period for Runcorn's Cheshire League side. They won three league champion-ships and other county honours.

However, their finest hour came in 1939 when they negotiated their way to a third round FA Cup clash with cup holders Preston North End. This was the time in cup history that a non-league side had been pitted against the cup holders. Despite leading against a team that inclu Bill Shankly, Runcorn eventually went down 4-2 in front of 10,000 Canal Street spectators. (*Author' Collection*)

ht: A rare view of
Search as he
kes a close range
against
nthorpe in the
Cup. The talented
tre forward
ays remained
l to his home
n club despite
rs from
balling giants
Arsenal.
n Cook)

Pride in the town football team is
celebrated in this trimmed bush at
the War Memorial Club in York
Street. Mr Stathers reshaped it
into the outline of the Cheshire
Senior Cup, recognising the club's
cup success. The Linnets won this
trophy on eleven occasions
between 1924 and 1989.
(Dave Thompson)

he 1960s the directors of
corn Football Club were
ed to acquire a new club
ctor, none other than
edian Ken Dodd. To Ken
d's left is George Woods,
rman of the club for a
ber of years.
icorn Weekly News)

Match programme for the Linnets' 1964 duel with Frickley Colliery. Runcorn were chasing for the championship at the time. (*Author's Collection*)

This photograph shows the team that won the Cheshire League in 1962. However, the mid-1970s to e[a]rly 1980s heralded the most successful period in the club's history. They won the NPL treble in 1980/81 [a]nd followed it up the following year by winning non-league football's top flight league, then called the Allia[nce] Premier League, now known as the conference. (*Runcorn Weekly News*)

Linnets reached the FA Trophy final at Wembley on three occasions between 1986 and 1994. They
e beaten to non-leagues premier prize on all three occasions. This picture shows Runcorn en route to
ther FA trophy final after a thrilling cup replay victory over Yeovil Town. (*Runcorn Weekly News*)

ht: Linnets' defender Jamie Bates receives the
94 'player of the year' award from supporters'
b chairman Noel Bell. The supporters' club
s formed in the 1930s and has always played
active role in supporting the Linnets. (*Dave
mpson*)

Runcorn AFC was also blighted by disasters off the field in the 1990s. The club's struggle to bring in greater gate receipts was made all the worse when a wall collapsed during a FA Cup first-round tie with Hull. Worse was to follow. This is the scene in 1994 when the club's main stand was destroyed in an arson attack. (*Dave Thompson*)

Alan Finley strikes on goal in this 1995 derby match against Altrincham. The Linnets played their last match at Canal Street in 2001. Following their move to the Halton Stadium they renamed themselves Runcorn FC Halton. (*Dave Thompson*)

Rugby League returned to Canal Street for a spell in the 1980s. Runcorn Highfield's short stay was a reminder of a century earlier when Runcorn was very much a rugby town. The team failed to flourish and became better known for its defeats and a players' strike. It was a far cry from 1907 when a Runcorn team beat the New Zealand team in front of over 10,000 local spectators. During that famous pioneering tour Runcorn was the only Northern Union rugby team to successfully prevent the New Zealanders from scoring. (*Runcorn Weekly News*)

...ny sporting clubs enjoyed social outings. These men are regulars of the Runcorn Bowls Club, posing for a ...stcard portrait to mark their club outing from the Bridge pub. The Ashridge Street pub was the HQ for the ...b and was reputed to have the best greens in Runcorn. (*Mildred Walker*)

Sir Frederick Norman bowls the first wood for the Runcorn Subscription Bowls Club at the opening in 1910 of their first green at Moughland Lane (to the rear of the fire station in Heath Road). The *Runcorn Weekly News* remarked on the club's establishment 'There is ample need for a club where men all shades of religion and politics can set aside their differences.' Fifteen years after the local industrialist opened the green it was forced to move to a new green on Moughland Lane, closer to Greenway Road (*Bill Leathwood*)

The last eight bowlers gather together for a photograph during the Runcorn Subscription Bowls Club 'Presidents Day' in 1929. The private members' club is still active today. (*Bill Leathwood*)

o-based games have always been popular in Runcorn and the town has a strong tradition of darts, bowls
l dominos. The darts league was once regarded as one of the best organised in the country. This is a
ture of darts league officials in the early 1960s. (*Dave Thompson*)

the 1990s the town also
duced a great boxing hero
Robin Reid. The Runcorn
ker won a bronze medal at
1992 Barcelona
mpics and was later
ded through a 22 fight
beaten run by promoter
nk Warren, resulting in
WBC world super-
ddleweight title in 1996.
d was not Runcorn's first
king hero: that honour
s to Harry Twist. Fighting
der the name of 'Young
ncorn' he made a name
himself in 1920s
nerica. The two-fisted
uler fought across the
A and the big-time
nerican promoters in
tham hired his services.
ncorn Weekly News)

A young Bold Street man made the sporting headlines in 1926 when he became both English Amateur and Wo Billiards Champion. Joe Earlam burst c to the English billiards scene after havi perfected his skills and reputation on t tables of the old Liberal Club in Regent Street. The streets of the town were lin with thousands of people when he returned from his world conquering triumphs. He became a professional bu his career seemed to nosedive soon afterwards. (*Peter Ainsworth, World Billiards*)

Another hero of the green baize, with a more lasting effect, is Runcorn-based pool star Sue Thompson. She has won the Ladies World Pool Championship on no fewer than four occasions and has been the fastest ladies pool player in the world since 1996. She still exhibits her potting skills all over the country and holds the 'speed' record for clearing all 15 balls in 37.7 seconds. (*Runcorn Weekly News*)